IMAGES
of America

FORT YELLOWSTONE

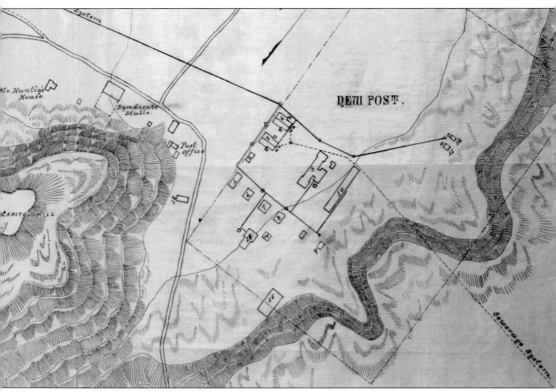

This 1894 map is one of the few maps that offers an overview of Mammoth Hot Springs and the arrangement of both Army posts. Camp Sheridan (1886–1890) is labeled "Old Post" and appears on the left side of the map. Fort Yellowstone (1891–1918), on the right, is identified as the "New Post." (Courtesy of Yellowstone National Park Archives.)

ON THE COVER: An unidentified photographer captured a sense of the military's eager spirit for protecting America's first national park in this image taken at the Upper Geyser Basin on August 23, 1893. (YELL 14418; courtesy of Yellowstone National Park Museum Collection.)

IMAGES
of America

FORT YELLOWSTONE

Elizabeth A. Watry and Lee H. Whittlesey

ARCADIA
PUBLISHING

Published by Arcadia Publishing
Charleston, South Carolina

Printed in the United States of America

Library of Congress Control Number: 2011938857

For all general information, please contact Arcadia Publishing:
Telephone 843-853-2070
Fax 843-853-0044
E-mail sales@arcadiapublishing.com
For customer service and orders:
Toll-Free 1-888-313-2665

Visit us on the Internet at www.arcadiapublishing.com

*To all the generations of military personnel who preserved and
protected the wonders of Yellowstone for future generations*

CONTENTS

ACKNOWLEDGMENTS

The authors would like to thank the Yellowstone National Park Museum Collection and Digital (online) Slide Collection, Yellowstone Gateway Museum, Yale Beinecke Library, University of Oregon, Bob Berry, Bill Arnold, and other private collectors for granting us permission to publish images from their archival repositories.

The images from Yellowstone National Park appear courtesy of the Yellowstone National Park Museum Collection (YNPMC) and the Yellowstone National Park Digital Slide File (YNPDSF). In addition, images from Yellowstone National Park Museum Collection Black Scrapbook No. 22 appear as (BS22).

INTRODUCTION

On August 17, 1886, Capt. Moses Harris rode into Mammoth Hot Springs with his command, Company M of the 1st US Cavalry, to assume administrative control of Yellowstone National Park. Less than two weeks earlier, an exasperated US Congress had given up on the idea of effective civilian administration of the park and declined to appropriate funding for its management and protection. The park's saving grace came from legislation that had been surprisingly passed without opposition or debate in 1883. Proposed by the Committee on Appropriations and amended by one of the park's most ardent supporters, Sen. George Graham Vest of Missouri, the rider stipulated the following: "The Secretary of War, upon the request of the Secretary of Interior, is hereby authorized and directed to make the necessary details of troops to prevent trespassers or intruders from entering the park for the purpose of destroying game or objects of curiosity therein, or for any purpose prohibited by law, and to remove such persons from the park if found therein." In the summer of 1886, Secretary of Interior Lucius Q.C. Lamar invoked that 1883 law, and on August 20, Captain Harris formally assumed responsibility for America's first national park. The Army's duty was expected to be temporary, but it would be 32 years later when the last troops rode out of the park—through Yellowstone's stone archway and into history.

Under Army administration, conditions in Yellowstone began to improve when the military's numbers and money made an immediate difference. Harris erected the eight initial buildings of "Camp Sheridan" just below the Mammoth terraces. He stationed men at six key locations in the park to enforce regulations, prevent vandalism, and watch for illegal hunters, arresting several in the first few years and making park visitors feel that the place was safe for tourism. His new oversight of hotel concessioners remedied problems and helped erase the public's (and Congress's) memory of corporate abuses in the preceding three years.

Under the Army, the previously stalled Yellowstone began to move forward. When lightning ignited forests, Captain Harris sent out the first federal wildland firefighters in US history. When vandals stole geyser specimens for souvenirs and scribbled and scratched their names on park natural objects, he and others caught them and marched them back to the scenes to scrub out their handiwork. And when Capt. George Anderson's men arrested a buffalo killer in 1894, the resulting publicity caused Congress to pass the nation's first federal wildlife protection statute.

Camp Sheridan soon became too small, especially as it became apparent that the Army's "temporary" duty was to be a long-term one. In 1891, Capt. George S. Anderson received permission and money to construct a permanent post. Starting at the south end of today's "parade ground" and building to the north, workmen erected 12 structures that year so that Anderson and his men could occupy them by November. The buildings included a guardhouse, a headquarters, two double officers' quarters, a commissary, storehouse, granary, bakery, troop barracks, cavalry stable, and two noncommissioned officers' residences. In 1894, workmen added a hospital, a hay shed, and a steward's quarters so that the post could hold one troop of soldiers, consisting of 60–100 men. Construction of Fort Yellowstone forever changed the face of the village of Mammoth and gave the settlement its distinct cultural identity, which the National Park Service still preserves today as a "cultural landscape."

Over time, more buildings were needed, as the post grew to accommodate two, three, and finally four troops. In 1897, workmen built two more officers' duplexes facing the parade ground, a second troop barracks, another cavalry stable, and two more noncommissioned officers' quarters. Construction continued nearly constantly until 1913, when the final building—the present Mammoth Chapel—was completed. During that period, the characteristic stone buildings were finished (all in 1909) along with a post exchange, more cavalry stables, a third large barracks (today's NPS administration building), and other buildings until the completed Fort Yellowstone held more than 60 structures. Many are no longer standing, but some 35 remain today.

Under the Army's continuing protection, stagecoach tourism—spearheaded by four transportation companies and dozens of independents with their hundreds of gaily bedecked horses—evolved into a smoothly functioning adventure that guided thousands of visitors through Yellowstone. This tourism was the backdrop for the Army's conversion of Mammoth and Fort Yellowstone from a frontier hardscrabble of log cabins into a picturesque, pastoral village that provided comfort in the midst of a wilderness, offered idyllic pleasure to the masses, and served as an inspirational, useful, and even patriotic park headquarters. In the park south of Mammoth, the Army built and manned "soldier stations" at numerous locations from which soldiers could patrol to protect thermal formations and monitor activities of visitors. It added 16 "snowshoe cabins" to the backcountry so that soldiers could watch the park for illegal hunters during all seasons. Occasionally, individual soldiers even dabbled in park interpretation and tour guiding (if they had been there long enough to become interested and learn the place), but the Army's presence was always more for protection than interpretation. Because of the Army's solving of the park's many initial problems, Yellowstone became a successful experiment in tourism by 1900 and a truly idyllic place for the rest of its stagecoach days.

At the same time that automobiles were admitted into Yellowstone (1915) and the United States was faced with the threat of World War I, the US Army made ready to leave its national park mission and to return to its historic function in the nation's Department of War. Congress created the new National Park Service in 1916, and the Army took the train out of Yellowstone. But impediments remained. Some members of Congress did not like the new government agency, so they cut off its money, and the Army was forced to return to the park for two more years. Finally in late 1918, the Army left the park for the second and final time.

The US Army truly left its mark in the first national park. It laid the groundwork for what later would become the National Park Service's headquarters and offices, it established a methodology for managing the park, and it even influenced the "look" of the later park rangers. Fort Yellowstone consisted of more than 60 buildings, and most of them remain in use today by the NPS. The Army's system of trails, its use of stations for patrol purposes, its enforcement of regulations and the generating of new ones, its cordiality to visitors, its oversight of concessioners, and its interest in managing park animals all remain today. In various forms, those ideas are now incorporated into the National Park Service's Divisions of Law Enforcement, Maintenance, Interpretation, Concessions Management, and the Yellowstone Center for Resources. Even the Army's uniform, with its "campaign hats," shoulder epaulets, badges, and leather, was essentially pressed into service in 1916 by the new National Park Service. Today's rangers still wear a "flat hat" that was and is modeled after the "campaign hat" of the post–Civil War Army.

In short, during its 32 years in the park, the Army created and emplaced a bigger-than-life legacy upon Yellowstone and upon today's National Park Service.

One

CAMP SHERIDAN

Prior to entry of the Army, Yellowstone National Park was managed by civilians who were overwhelmed by lack of money, staff, and the challenges of dealing with a huge, remote landmass. Early superintendents, such as Philetus Norris, were besieged with problems but did the best they could with what they had. Frustrated by the problems, Congress angrily cut off all money to these administrators, resulting in the Army's takeover of the park in August 1886.

Initially, the new troops found the place almost deserted because the 10 assistant superintendents, knowing they would not be paid, abandoned their posts. Only the previous superintendent remained in place to show Capt. Moses Harris his new domain. Harris stationed troops at six locations around the park and began almost at once to build a primitive post. Named "Camp Sheridan," it was completed enough by November to give the soldiers a place to stay for what turned into the legendarily cold winter of 1886–1887.

Although Camp Sheridan became too small within five years, many of its old buildings remained on the site until at least 1915 with several lasting even longer. The Army needed the extra housing and storage space even after the newer post, Fort Yellowstone, was completed.

After serving in the Civil War and working a brief, but profitable, stint in the real estate business, Philetus Walter Norris became Yellowstone's second superintendent in April 1877. Somewhat of a renaissance man, he administered the park with the regimentation of a military man, the curiosity of a scientist, the practicality of a pioneer, and the heart of a true explorer. This image was taken around 1878. (02959; courtesy of YNPDSF.)

After the Nez Perce War in the summer of 1877 and the ensuing flight of the Nez Perce through the park, threatening the lives of several tourists, Norris was especially concerned about Indian attacks. He chose Mammoth Hot Springs as his headquarters and in 1879 constructed this building, the Norris Blockhouse (pictured around 188), which served as the park's first formal administrative building. (YELL 50779; courtesy of YNPMC.)

Sitting high atop Capitol Hill, the blockhouse afforded Norris the security of a 360-degree vantage point of Mammoth Hot Springs. From here, Norris would produce some of the park's earliest official Reports to the Secretary of Interior, in which he cataloged his monumental efforts to undertake road and building construction and to studiously investigate the park's human and natural history. (E.W. Kelley stereoview; courtesy of Bob Berry.)

Norris included this drawing in his annual Report to the Secretary of Interior 1880 as the frontispiece. In the center on what appears to be a mound in relation to the larger surrounding mountains is Norris's blockhouse proudly flying the US flag. Superintendent from 1877 until 1882, Norris was followed by several, mostly ineffectual, civilian superintendents. (Courtesy of Montana State University Library infoweb.)

This rare B.W. Kilburn stereoview captured what is probably the hastily set up camp of Capt. Moses Harris and Company M, 1st US Cavalry, after their arrival in Yellowstone on August 17, 1886. Camp was probably set up here at Mammoth for its closeness to water and also to announce the military presence and herald that order would follow. (Kilburn stereoview 4274; courtesy Bob Berry.)

4274. Mammoth Hot Springs, Yellowstone National Park. U. S. A

Another rare Kilburn stereoview shows the opposite viewpoint of the presumed 1886 cavalry camp (upper left) from the terraces. Note the Cottage Hotel, built in 1885 (upper left just beyond the camp), and the massive National Hotel, even then becoming known as Mammoth Hot Springs Hotel (built 1883–1886). (Kilburn stereoview 4278; courtesy of Bob Berry.)

4278. Hotel Plateau. Yellowstone National Park.

12

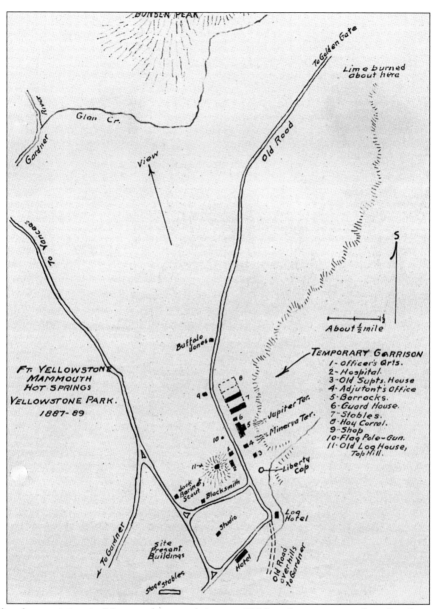

Shortly after arriving in Mammoth in mid-August 1886 and receiving orders that he and his one troop of cavalry were expected to stay through the winter, Captain Harris employed a 17-man crew of carpenters and a 10-man crew working the sawmill to begin construction of Camp Sheridan. The first buildings erected were the barracks and officers' quarters, with other buildings constructed shortly thereafter. Until the establishment of Fort Yellowstone, the park was administered year round by one troop of cavalry, which consisted of less than 40 men; thus, the size of the camp facilities was rather small by military standards. This map that George Tutherly, son of 1st Lt. Herbert E. Tutherly, drew from memory in 1926 shows the locations of the principle structures at Camp Sheridan. One of the problems inherent with relying on recollections and memoirs as historical tools is evidenced here; Tutherly's map of the camp that he dated as 1886–1889 and shows Buffalo Jones's house and corral, which did not exist until 1902. ("From the Writings of George Tutherly"; courtesy YNP Library Manuscript Collection.)

This overview of Camp Sheridan from the north with Marble Terrace to the left looks down on the Army barns and utility buildings as they appeared in 1895. At top center of the photograph, note Norris's blockhouse sporting a prominent spot on top of Capitol Hill. (BS22, photograph 3-JN; courtesy of YNPMC.)

Serving as officer's quarters, the frame structure at bottom center of this c. 1900 photograph was dubbed the "Beehive," presumably because of the steady buzz of activity in and around that building. The barracks building shown on the map on the next page is the long building to the left of the Beehive. (YELL 302854; courtesy of YNPMC.)

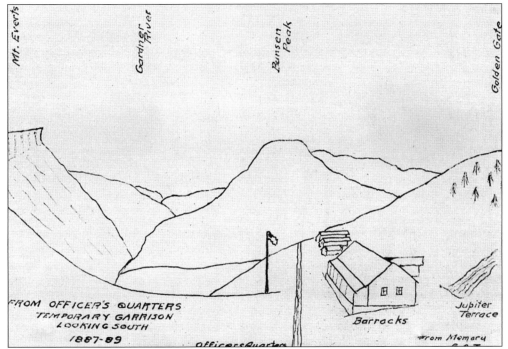

George Tutherly's map drawing here shows the locations of the barracks and the officers' quarters looking south. ("From the Writings of George Tutherly"; courtesy YNP Library Manuscript Collection.)

In this view from sometime between 1908 and 1913, the Reservoir Spring/Cavern Terrace House, listed as the "old superintendent's house" on Tutherly's map above, stands at the bottom of the Mammoth Hot Springs Terraces on the right side of the photograph around 1908–1913. The former adjutant's office is the building on the left. The Beehive house is farther left and out of view. (Courtesy of Bill Arnold.)

Consistent with the park's practice for reuse of old buildings, the Reservoir Spring/Cavern Terrace house became housing for several generations of park employees until it was torn down in 1937. Some of the dwelling's better-known residents included Chester Lindsley, who would later become the park's first acting superintendent under the National Park Service administration, and famed park ranger Harry Trischman. (Courtesy of Bill Arnold.)

Called the "Reservoir Spring/Cavern Terrace House," because it was built between present-day Reservoir Spring to its south and Cavern Terrace to its north, the Lindsley house went through several modifications and additions, including several outbuildings visible here. This photograph (1908–1913) from the back of the house displays a commanding view of Mammoth Hot Springs village that the residents surely enjoyed. (Courtesy of Bill Arnold.)

Two

WELL APPOINTED AND SETTLED

Notwithstanding the Army's initial plans, Camp Sheridan became too small within five years. On May 11, 1891, "Special Orders No. 45" gave acting park superintendent George S. Anderson the authority to construct a new military post that would soon be named "Fort Yellowstone." Construction at this "new post," as many soldiers called it, lasted for nearly 22 years.

Because the main road from Gardiner, Montana, then entered Mammoth village from the south (by ascending through today's lower NPS housing area), Captain Anderson's workmen erected the fort from south to north. The Army's police function required that a guardhouse be built first, which was followed by a superintendent's office and then soldiers' housing. Twelve buildings were completed and occupied by November 1891 and included the following: a guardhouse, a headquarters, two double officers' quarters, a commissary, storehouse, granary, bakery, troop barracks, cavalry stable, and two noncommissioned officers' residences. Three more buildings were added in 1894 and 1893, including a 10-bed hospital, a two-story residence for the hospital steward, and a large hay shed. The US judge's stone house was also built in the latter year, far to the west.

This was deemed enough for a one-troop fort, but the fort would soon grow, eventually housing four troops. (Although full troop strength was 100 men, research shows that no troop at Fort Yellowstone ever contained more than 81 men.) Accordingly, workmen constructed (in 1897) a second troop barracks, another cavalry stable, two more noncommissioned officers' quarters, and two more officers' duplexes.

By this time, the four officers' duplexes all faced what was becoming known as the "parade ground" because the Army used it for drilling and ceremonial activities.

Construction at Fort Yellowstone continued until 1913, when the final building—today's Mammoth Chapel—was finished. Of the more than 60 original Fort Yellowstone buildings, only about 35 remain today at Mammoth. Cost for the fort came to about $552,000 with an additional $75,000 for utilities. After adding another $75,000 for improvements to the parade ground, the grand total invested in the fort by Department of War was about $700,000.

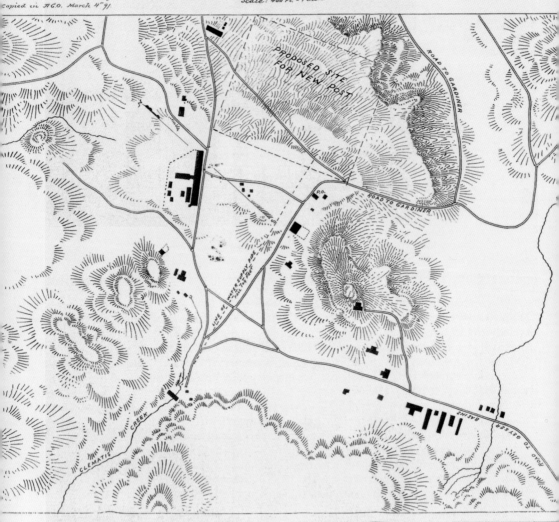

Department of Interior
February 27 1891
Approved:
John W. Noble
Secretary

Copied in A.G.O. March 4th 91

MAP OF
MAMMOTH HOT SPRINGS
Yellowstone National Park
Scale: 400 Ft. = 1 inch

With no end in sight to the Army's duty in Yellowstone, the secretary of war submitted a proposal to erect a permanent post in 1890. Authorization to construct Fort Yellowstone was received in early 1891 after the site chosen by the acting superintendent Capt. Frazier A. Boutelle (1889–1891) was approved by the Department of Interior. Construction of the "new post" began in April and utilized civilian contractors under the watchful eye of Capt. George S. Anderson, who had replaced Boutelle in February. The first buildings, which included two double officers' quarters, a troop barracks, a guardhouse, an administrative building, a commissary storehouse, quartermaster storehouse, a granary, a bakery, a set of cavalry stables, two sets of quarters for noncommissioned officers, and a root house, were ready for occupancy by November. Within the next six years, the hospital, hospital steward's quarters, a hay shed, an additional barracks, and two more double officers' quarters were erected. The map is dated February 27, 1891. (Courtesy of YNP Library.)

18

This view from the top of Capitol Hill reveals Fort Yellowstone in its embryonic stages of construction around 1894. (YELL 10328; courtesy of YNPMC.)

The fort's layout, in typical military fashion of buildings standing side by side, reminded many visitors that Yellowstone National Park was the domain of the US government. This c. 1897–1899 image was most likely taken by Chester Lindsley, who later became the first acting superintendent of Yellowstone for the National Park Service in 1916. (Courtesy of Bill Arnold.)

The cannon situated atop Capitol Hill overlooking Fort Yellowstone in this c. 1903 image was present for show, not defense. The nightly firing of the cannon as a salute to sundown became a Yellowstone tradition fondly recalled by visitors. The sundown cannon fired blanks for this purpose. (09610; courtesy of YNPDSF.)

One of Hiram Chittenden's clerks, A.L. Noyes, took this photograph in 1902. The buildings' white exteriors and red roofs presented a dramatic if austere scene for visitors arriving via horse-drawn wagons and coaches. Wagons that can be see here are work vehicles of the Army and probably its road engineers. (YELL 109620; courtesy of YNPMC.)

The Army's guardhouse, built in 1891 and pictured here around 1898, was the first building that visitors would see as they approached Mammoth Hot Springs via the road from Gardiner. (YELL 11497; courtesy of YNPMC.)

Frank J. Haynes, the park's official photographer, erected the residence at right in 1885. Located directly across from the Mammoth Hotel, it doubled as a studio and sales shop. In the background, the four double officers' quarters presented a stately appearance in this c. 1900 photograph. (YELL 9448; courtesy of YNPMC.)

Hay that was thrown upon the ground by the Army plus a grassy parade ground in front of the duplex officers' quarters drew in hungry deer during the winter season in the early 1900s, just as natural grass sometimes does today. Note the guy-wired iron flagstaff that was erected in 1900. (Courtesy of Bill Arnold.)

Replacing the original 1891 flagstaff in 1900, the new iron, stepped-style staff was anchored in concrete and rigged in a manner typical of Army posts during that time. Some reports claimed that the staff was 75 feet high, while others recorded it as 100 feet. Either way, Marguerite Lindsley (top of ladder) and her playmates found the staff a great place to play. (Courtesy of Bill Arnold.)

The area used by the Army for drills and as a parade ground was located between the Mammoth Hot Springs Hotel and the officers' quarters. Originally barren and sandy, the parade ground was a dusty spot until 1895, when Captain Anderson experimented with planting grass, which was made even more successful by Army engineer Chittenden in 1901–1902. In this c. 1914 image, Army troops gather on the parade ground. (13222; courtesy of YNPDSF.)

In 1902, Army engineer Hiram Chittenden electrified all of the buildings in Mammoth as well as the main thoroughfare and parade ground. This photograph was probably taken on the very first night that the streetlights were illuminated on November 13, 1902. Previously, outdoor lights at Mammoth were gas-powered. (YELL 606; courtesy of YNPMC.)

By 1908, the drill and parade ground experiment of planting grass was enduring, which made it a pleasant place for soldiers to gather for a sunny afternoon of leisure. Note the cannons in the far left background. This undated photograph must have been taken between 1897 and 1909, because the stone buildings of 1909 were not yet present and the two officers' duplexes were completed in 1897. (YELL 36989; courtesy of YNPMC.)

In this c. 1912 image, the two-troop bachelor officers' quarters (stone building at front center) and the enlisted men's quarters (stone building at far left) complement the orderly line up of military residences along Officers' Row. There were no large trees yet in front of the residences, because cottonwoods planted as early as 1895 in front of the first two duplexes failed to establish. A planting in the mid-1920s succeeded, and those cottonwoods remain today. (YELL 30311; courtesy of YNPMC.)

Other government buildings at Mammoth that were notable by the time this 1910 postcard was published included the US Weather Bureau (square building at front left) and the US Engineer's House (partly cropped out at bottom center, built 1902). The US Engineer's Office, with its hipped roof (just above the house, built 1903), became known as the Pagoda. (10645; courtesy NPDSF.)

Built in 1903, the US Weather Bureau (gone today) was a two-story, Colonial-styled structure that acting superintendent Major Pitcher referred to as "quite a handsome frame building" in his Report to the Secretary of Interior 1903. The weather at Mammoth was recorded here from 1903 until around 1948 and continues today elsewhere. The building was torn down in the 1960s after serving as employee housing. This photograph was taken in 1917. (BS22, photograph 2G-43; courtesy of YNPMC.)

Ranking as a captain in the US Army Corps of Engineers, Hiram Chittenden apparently believed that he should have a headquarters befitting an officer. In late 1902, he requested and was granted authorization to construct this two-story stone office building (pictured in 1917), which he completed in 1903. By July 1903, Chittenden was requesting top-quality furnishings to complement his fine new building. (BS22, photograph 2G-41; courtesy of YNPMC.)

Before building his office, Chittenden asked for permission to build a residence for himself. In the plans sent to Washington, he called the house "the residence of Captain H.M. Chittenden." His proposal was approved, but with the name changed to "the residence of the U.S. Engineer officer." Ironically, the building, completed by November 1902 and shown here in 1917, is today referred to as the Chittenden house. (BS22 photograph 2G-35; courtesy of YNPMC.)

This two-story stone structure was built in 1909 to house the Army's unmarried officers and so became known as the "Bachelor Officers' Quarters," or BOQ. It contained apartments for six single officers and an officers' mess. Pictured here in 1917, today the building houses the National Park Service's Mammoth Albright Visitors Center, the Yellowstone Association bookstore, and a small museum that interprets the early exploration of Yellowstone. (BS22, photograph 2G-49; courtesy of YNPMC.)

Designed to house two officers and their families, the first two (most southerly) of these frame buildings with tin roofs were built in 1891, and another two (most northerly shown here) were erected in 1897. The living space in each half of the duplex included a parlor, dining room, kitchen, four bedrooms, pantries, full attic, partial basement, and closets. This photograph was taken in 1917. (BS22, photograph 2G-57; courtesy of YNPMC.)

Pictured in 1917, this stone residence, called the "Double Captain's Quarters," was built in 1909 to house two officers and their families. Modern in contrast to its remoteness, each half of it contained three water closets (toilets), two washbasins, two wash sinks, two laundry tubs, and two bathtubs. Its defining characteristic was a front porch on the south side, unlike all its neighbors, which contained front porches on their west sides. (BS22, photograph 2G-50; courtesy of YNPMC.)

Constructed as the residence for the superintendent in 1909, this building is the only building in Fort Yellowstone that has been continually used for its original purpose. Because the commander of the park was expected to entertain guests, this residence contained eight bedrooms, four water closets, three bathtubs, and four more rooms in the attic. (BS22, photograph 2G-55; courtesy of YNPMC.)

Four of these frame 1.5-story buildings were constructed to house noncommissioned officers (corporals and sergeants). Two were completed 1891 (today's most southerly and most northerly buildings), and the two in the middle were completed in 1897. Rather smallish, their floor plan consisted of a parlor, dining room, pantry, kitchen, and one bedroom. Pictured here in 1917, they continue to be used as residences today. (BS22, photograph 2G-101; courtesy of YNPMC.)

Completed in 1897 at a cost of $13,187, this 6,520-square-foot troop barracks included two dormitories that would accommodate 68 men, the company store, a kitchen and pantry, a cook's room, a day room, an orderly room, a lavatory, and a mess room. Today, this building provides offices for the National Park Service's Yellowstone Center for Resources. (BS22, photograph 2G-85; courtesy of YNPMC.)

This 1909 photograph shows the construction of the double cavalry barracks that was designed to accommodate 200 men. When it was completed at a cost of $95,469, this barracks for the enlisted men was the largest building at Fort Yellowstone. (Courtesy of Clayton P. Daugherty.)

The interior furnishings of the double cavalry barracks included wall lockers, bunks, footlockers, and rifle racks. This photograph was taken in 1917. Its interior was completely remodeled in 2004–2006, and today it is used as the park's main administration building by the National Park Service. (BS22, photograph 2G-87; courtesy of YNPMC.)

The Army commissary and office occupied this building following its completion on December 5, 1891 (shown here in 1917). The floor plan consisted of a large storeroom, an office, and an issue room. Today, it is used as a duplex residence. (BS22, photograph 2G-47; courtesy of YNPMC.)

This building (pictured in 1917) is virtually identical to the commissary store and office. Also completed in 1891, this structure originally served as the quartermaster's storehouse and office, where supplies for the commisary were kept. As with its twin, this building was later converted to a duplex residence. (BS22, photograph 2G-60; courtesy of YNPMC.)

Information on the first post exchange at Fort Yellowstone is scant, other than it contained of a store and a canteen and was merely a converted dwelling. Used for soldiers' recreational activities, the structure shown here in 1917—the second post exchange—appears to be more than a one-story wood frame building. Completed in 1905, it contained at least a billiard room, a reading room, and a gymnasium among its many rooms. (BS22, photograph 2G-53; courtesy of YNPMC.)

With a capacity for 94 horses, this two-story cavalry stable was constructed in 1909. While the horse stalls occupied the first floor, a hayloft and granary dominated the second floor. Hay could be lifted to its second story via a block-and-tackle, which is shown here occurring in 1917. Today, this building is used as the National Park Service's Communications Center and Chief Ranger's Office. (BS22, photograph 2G-8; courtesy of YNPMC.)

Presenting a commanding presence of the military, the guardhouse contained three jail cells as well as an officer's room and a guardroom. From 1891 through the rest of the park's stagecoach era, it was the first building that most visitors saw when they entered the village, because the road from north entrance from Gardiner, Montana, entered Mammoth at this point. This photograph was taken in 1904. (YELL 171148; courtesy of YNPMC.)

After Congress passed the Lacey Act in 1894, giving the Army legal authority to enforce a no-hunting law in Yellowstone, visitors were required to stop at the guardhouse to register their names and have their guns sealed before traveling farther into the park. The armed soldier standing on the corner made compliance mandatory. (YELL 171148; courtesy of YNPMC.)

After an inspection in 1909, the original Fort Yellowstone guardhouse was condemned and ordered to be "broken up." However, following construction of a new guardhouse in 1911, this building was used as an ordnance storehouse. Pictured here around 1895, the former guardhouse is still in use today as a residence. (15338; courtesy of YNPDSF.)

The concrete 1.5-story guardhouse (jail) with red clay tile roof, was constructed in 1911. Consistent with a prison structure, bars embedded in the cement covered the wooden double-hung windows in the cells and toilet. This photograph was taken in 1917. Today, remodeled and upgraded, this building is still used as a jail by the National Park Service. (BS22, photograph 2G-59; courtesy of YNPMC.)

Fort Yellowstone's first hospital at Mammoth was constructed in 1894 and is pictured here around 1895. The Army previously had a hospital at Camp Sheridan. This hospital, which had 10 beds, offered medical services to visitors as well as military personnel and their families. (15337; courtesy of YNPDSF.)

Following the construction of Fort Yellowstone's second hospital in 1911, the first hospital building, shown here in 1917, was used as office space by the Army acting superintendent. (BS22, photograph 2G-44; courtesy of YNPMC.)

Built in the spring of 1894, this tin-roofed frame house, pictured in 1917, served as the hospital steward's quarters. In 1901, a woman visitor in need of medical attention was escorted to this residence by local tour guide G.L. Henderson, where they found the steward and his family "out on the lawn, under the shade of a tree," observing the Sabbath. (BS22, photograph 2G-54; courtesy of YNPMC.)

The Army's second hospital at Fort Yellowstone hospital (third including Camp Sheridan's) was a stone structure located next to the chapel. Completed in 1911 and shown here in 1917, this hospital served park residents and visitors until it was torn down in 1965 due to extensive structural damage caused by the 1959 Hebgen Lake earthquake. (BS22, photograph 2G-51; courtesy of YNPMC.)

In the days before refrigeration, soldiers cut blocks of ice from nearby lakes, packed the blocks in sawdust, and stored them in this dirt-floored log building at old Camp Sheridan. Pictured here sometime before 1909, this 12-by-40-foot icehouse had a capacity of 30 tons of ice. (BS22, photograph 2G-28; courtesy of YNPMC.)

Pictured in 1917, the bakery was probably as essential for the sustainability of the troops as was housing. As such, it was constructed in the fort's first phase of construction during 1891. With his workroom containing merely a kneading table, a sink, a storeroom, and two ovens, the post baker reportedly could supply 250 rations per day in 1899. (BS22, photograph 2G-84; courtesy of YNPMC.)

In 1917 when this photograph was taken, this building was listed as being used as a blacksmith shop. Its earlier purposes included the troops' workshop and as a paint shop. Today, it is used for storage. (BS22, photograph 2G-96; courtesy of YNPMC.)

The hospital annex, shown here in 1917, was constructed in 1909 to serve as living quarters for soldiers on hospital duty. The one-story building could house 12 men. As with many of the buildings at Fort Yellowstone, its stoves were used for heat. After being used as a warehouse, the annex was transformed into employee housing. (BS22, photograph 2G-77; courtesy of YNPMC.)

These small coal sheds were representative of numerous such sheds that stored the valuable fuel, which kept soldiers and their families warm during Yellowstone's long and cold winters. Long after many of the residences had been converted to fuel oil, many of these sheds still existed, as shown in this 1917 image. Like most of the fort's buildings, they were probably utilized for other purposes and eventually torn down. (BS22, photograph 2G-56; Courtesy of YNPMC.)

This 12-by-26-foot root cellar with earthen floor and roof was built in 1891 at a cost of $75.90. Its semi-subterranean location in the east base of Capitol Hill made it a likely structure to be used as an ordnance dugout, as evidenced by the "Danger No Smoking" sign posted on the door in this 1917 photograph. But, at times, it was also used to store hay. (BS22, photograph2G-76; courtesy of YNPMC.)

Built into the east base of Capitol Hill, this structure originally served as the commissary root cellar after it was constructed in 1909. Observing the bars on the door and the sandbags flanking its concrete exterior in this 1917 image, one can surmise that this, too, was used at some point as an ordnance dugout, although complete records are lacking. (BS22, photograph 2G-46; courtesy of YNPMC.)

Surveying buildings in 1917 that the new NPS was inheriting, park photographer Jack Haynes identified this as the "Scouts' Bunkhouse." However, it resembles the old hospital morgue built in 1898, so probably that morgue was moved to this site for reuse as a bunkhouse. As this building no longer stands, its history may remain mysterious, but probably it housed the Army's civilian scouts who hunted poachers. (BS22, photograph 2G-118; courtesy of YNPMC.)

Upon his return for a second term of duty in Yellowstone in 1899, Hiram Chittenden erected these buildings from which to conduct his road-construction operations and to house his crews. While the buildings were simple in design, the elk-antler fence—probably inspired by photographer F.J. Haynes's similar fence—offered a pleasant ambiance to the complex. The sign above the center door in this c. 1900 image read, "U.S. Road Dept. General Office." (BS22, photograph AE-134; courtesy of YNPMC.)

Despite the Army's diligence in preventing poaching, illegal hunters reduced the bison population to about 25 animals by around 1900. In 1902, Captain Pitcher was given funding to purchase additional bison to help replenish the herd, hire buffalo keeper Charles J. "Buffalo" Jones, and construct this house and corral for that purpose. It served briefly as a "buffalo museum" during the 1920s and was torn down in 1936. This photograph was taken in 1917. (BS22; photograph 2G-25; courtesy of YNPMC.)

Following authorization and appointment of a US commissioner (judge) for Yellowstone in 1894, this two-story stone building pictured in 1917 was constructed to serve as residence, office, and jail. The office and jail were on the first floor and the residence on the second floor. Judge John W. Meldrum, Yellowstone's first US commissioner, lived and worked here for over 40 years. (YELL 30365; courtesy of YNPMC.)

Until the early 1900s, it was not War Department policy to erect or maintain chapels at every Army post. Judge Meldrum was instrumental in getting this charming sandstone structure erected in 1912 and opened in 1913. Pictured in 1917, the chapel has a pitched, slate-shingled roof supported by wooden trussed arches. (BS22, photograph 2G-52; courtesy of YNPMC.)

Three

A Soldier's Life

The Army's appointed mission at Fort Yellowstone has been referred to its "most unusual assignment," because of its accompanying responsibilities involving protecting a national park. This meant that the Army reported to two masters: the Department of War for military duties and the Department of Interior for park duties. The unusual dichotomy made life at the fort different from other posts around the American West.

Some duties were the same: guard duty, kitchen police, target practice, patrols (on horseback for much of the year but on skis in winter), fatigue (work details), and occasionally chasing deserters. Just as occurred at other posts, scheduled military activities of each day included reveille, retreat, stable call, sick call, inspections, ceremonial duties, and tattoo. However, drills and maneuvers were more restricted at Fort Yellowstone than other posts because of the Army's national park duties: pursuing poachers, fighting forest fires, patrolling roads and geyser basins, recording visitors in and out, sealing tourists' weapons and inspecting them along the way, and even occasionally serving as guides for visitors. This last duty was always limited to soldiers who had been in Yellowstone awhile and had an interest in doing it, and it was officially prohibited by specific orders during the latter years of the Army's presence. Most of the Army's functions in Yellowstone were protective and not interpretive.

Enlisted men resided in Army barracks, ate in large mess halls, and got paid only $13 per month. But clothing was furnished, some adventure was guaranteed, and there were no worries about unemployment.

Did soldiers like the duty? That was a mixed reaction; some did, and some did not. Park guide G.L. Henderson believed in 1889 that "the soldiers do not like this new function of preserving a national park. They say it is not a soldier's work, but Captain Harris has proved there is a good use to which an Army may be put even in time of peace." Notwithstanding this statement, some soldiers loved Fort Yellowstone, considering it idyllic. A good number of them made the transition to ranger when the Army left the park in 1918.

The interior of this troops' barracks appeared as orderly in this c. 1905 image as the exterior of Fort Yellowstone. As can be seen here, soldiers were supplied with the bare necessities such as an iron framed bed, a footlocker, a mattress, a few blankets, and pillows. The stove in the center of the room heated the dormitory-style room. (14309; courtesy of YNPDSF.)

On July 18, 1911, a fire broke out in the Double Cavalry Barracks, and a portion of the building was severely damaged. Troops F and G of the 1st Cavalry were occupying the barracks at the time of fire. However, the only injury was a soldier fighting the fire, who broke through the floor and fell three stories. (YELL 7973; courtesy of YNPMC.)

In this rare 1902–1904 real-photo postcard, these unidentified soldiers appear to be sporting the latest hairstyle (parted on the left or center) as they gathered for this group photograph in front of the troop barracks. Perhaps they all sent a copy home to friends and family. (Courtesy of Bob Berry.)

These soldiers may be leaving for patrol duty. It is somewhat possible to date this photograph because of the building's number 38 at the top center. That was the number of the Troop Workshops building, built in 1901, and the location of this image. The men are wearing khaki uniforms, indicating that the photograph can be no older than 1902–1904, when the Army changed uniforms from the frontier "blues." (Courtesy of Bob Berry.)

Pvt. Joseph Sissenwine (born in Rockville Center, New York, in 1888; discharged 1912) was a member of Troop G, 5th Cavalry, while he was at Fort Yellowstone. This formal studio portrait of Pvt. Joseph Sissenwine was taken sometime between 1909 and 1911 while he was stationed at Fort Yellowstone. (Courtesy of Judith Anderson.)

Pvt. Joseph Sissenwine sits proudly on horseback at Fort Yellowstone's first cavalry stable (today's park carpentry shop), in March 1909. Descendant Judith Anderson, of Minneapolis, says enlistment in the Army was an expedited route to citizenship for Sissenwine. (Courtesy of Judith Anderson.)

Taken at Fort Yellowstone March 1909.

In this 1909–1911 snapshot, two soldiers pose during a "fatigue" assignment, which is a normal work detail. Pvt. Joseph Sissenwine is at right, the second man is unidentified, and the park location is unknown but probably was at Camp Sheridan. (Courtesy of Judith Anderson.)

When he enlisted in the Army, Herbert Angelo was 22 years old and listed his occupation as farmer. Apparently enthralled with his exciting new profession, Angelo kept a 145-page diary of his tour of duty with Uncle Sam, of which 67 pages were devoted to his time in Yellowstone. This photograph was taken around 1901. (14316; courtesy of YNPDSF.)

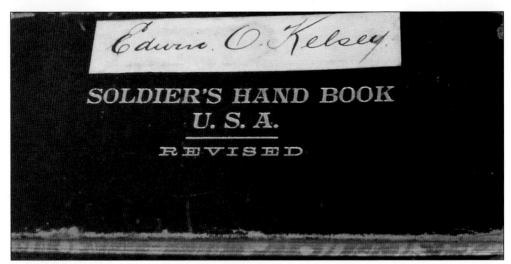

Edwin O. Kelsey (signature)

SOLDIER'S HAND BOOK
U. S. A.
REVISED

Edwin O. Kelsey served in Yellowstone in 1898. In a collection of letters to his niece, Kelsey left a wonderful record of his impressions of his time patrolling the wilderness areas of the park. Like all military personnel, he was issued a soldier's handbook, which contained all the rules, regulations, and instructions applicable to duty at Fort Yellowstone. (YELL 90960; courtesy of YNPMC.)

From the ongoing construction behind this soldier, it is evident that this photograph was taken in 1909 just as the bachelor officers' quarters and two other stone residences were being built at Mammoth. This soldier may be just arriving from another post, as he is wearing a dress uniform, which was not typical issue at Fort Yellowstone. (Courtesy of Randy Ingersoll.)

An Army machine-gun platoon lines up for a drill on the Mammoth parade ground with two mounted machine guns and cavalry troops at attention. This photograph was probably taken during the winter of 1902–1903, because the F. Jay Haynes house, moved to this site in October, can be seen at rear and because the troops were still wearing blue uniforms, which became khakis at the fort by 1904. (YELL 36930-3; courtesy of YNPMC.)

Jonathan M. Wainwright was a second lieutenant assigned to Fort Yellowstone in 1910, when this photograph was taken of a guard-mount ceremony. Commanding the machine-gun platoon, he also served as ordnance officer and signal officer. During World War II, he was forced to surrender Corregidor to the Japanese in 1942. After spending three years as a prisoner of war, Wainwright returned home a hero and participated in the Axis's official surrender in 1945. (YELL 36941-1; courtesy of YNPMC.)

An Army machine-gun platoon, possibly Wainwright's squad, is shown here in or about 1910 on the Mammoth parade ground, with the first Mammoth Hot Springs Hotel in the background. (YELL 9741; courtesy of YNPMC.)

Any photograph of sabers at Fort Yellowstone is rare, and in this undated image a soldier holds *two* of them. Although soldiers were issued sabers in addition to standard firearms, sabers were rarely used for defense after the Civil War. By the time of this soldier's duty in Yellowstone, sabers largely added only a bit of pageantry to the military's appearance. (Courtesy of Bill Arnold.)

Here is another rare glimpse of a detachment of saber soldiers performing a saber drill at the barracks that houses today's Yellowstone Center for Resources. Equally rare is any view of the building at far left, which was the first post exchange, or canteen, that stood here prior to construction of the present canteen in 1905. Winter or summer, soldier drills were a year round requirement in the military. Many visitors to Yellowstone were thrilled when they happened upon the flash and flair of a saber drill. (Courtesy of Bill Arnold.)

With rugged Mount Everts in the background, this cavalry drill team with all-white horses presented a striking scene of military poise in a 1904 H.C. White stereoview. B.L. Singly was the photographer who captured this special moment for all time, at a location east of Fort Yellowstone. (Courtesy of Bob Berry.)

Cavalry drills and other horseback events always seemed to draw a crowd, as the large gathering of people on the porch of the bachelor officers' quarters indicates in this rollicking image taken around 1910. (YELL 3693; courtesy of YNPMC.)

Having their horses run and jump over various heights of fences was one of the types of cavalry drills at Fort Yellowstone. Note that nearly all of the onlookers in this photograph have their legs raised in a crooked stance similar to the horse's leg, perhaps to "help" the horse kick high. (YELL 9743; courtesy of YNPMC.)

Acting superintendent Col. Lloyd M. Brett, probably second from left, supervised this rifle range practice session sometime around 1910–1916. According to historian Aubrey Haines, the first rifle range was on Elk Plaza, a mile north of the fort, but it was replaced sometime after 1900 by a more adequate setting at the mouth of the Gardner River. (11551; courtesy of YNPDSF.)

This c. 1910 view of an Army machine-gun squad was photographed near one of the cavalry stables at Mammoth. The man with his knee on the ammunition box has been identified as Trumpeter Conquette. John Mason is either standing or at the trigger. Others are unidentified. (YELL 9742; courtesy of YNPMC.)

Summer brought a lot of visitors to Yellowstone. Accordingly, the Army supplied extra troops to help with patrols. While the occasion of this 1912 photograph at Gardiner Depot is not known, more than likely it is the arrival or departure of a seasonal supply of soldiers. At rear is the north boundary fence, erected by Army engineer Chittenden in 1903. (YELL 142455; courtesy of YNPMC.)

A large group of soldiers of the 18th Infantry gathers in front of Old Faithful Geyser in this 1912 image. Just as visitors found it exciting to pose in front of the icon of Yellowstone, so too was it a thrill for the seasonal infantry that were brought in to help police the park during the summer. (YELL 142457; courtesy of YNPMC.)

Acting superintendent Col. Lloyd M. Brett, at far left, is leading a group of marching soldiers through the Firehole Basin in this c. 1910 image. The man walking next to Brett appears to be carrying a piece of road-survey equipment. (YELL 142458; courtesy of YNPMC.)

Troop F, 1st US Cavalry, gathered in front of the stone, two-troop barracks (today's administration building) for this 1913 group photograph. Note the soldier at far right standing at attention with his saber drawn, as well as the men sitting in the front rows with sabers. (YELL 90106; courtesy of YNPMC.)

During the summer, mounted soldiers like this one patrolled all park roads, geyser basins, and other points of interest to protect Yellowstone's natural features from vandalism and pilfering. Some of the incidents they encountered involved visitors chipping off pieces of geyser cones and campers failing to extinguish their fires. (03010; courtesy of YNPDSF.)

While most soldiers were stationed in the geyser basins to prevent vandalism, fires, and poaching and to protect visitors from injury, a few chose to be more proactive with their assignments and provide a bit of interpretation for interested visitors. This soldier, pictured before 1904, seems to be gesturing animatedly, explaining the workings of Giant Geyser to an interested onlooker. At rear, a uniformed concessioner tour guide wearing an identifiable square hat walks away. (09603; courtesy of YNPDSF.)

Acting superintendent Capt. Frazier A. Boutelle (1889–1891) spent some time in the fall of 1890 exploring Yellowstone. While most of the photographs in his collection list Boutelle as the photographer, this image of several people at Excelsior Geyser on September 19 was taken by Walter Weed, a USGS geologist who studied geysers that summer. The man standing at far left is probably Boutelle. (PH119-105; courtesy University of Oregon.)

Perhaps the thrill of being close to danger attracted this group of soldiers to pose for the camera, sometime after 1902, standing quite close to a boiling hot spring. Today's park regulations often prohibit such close approaches to hot springs. (YELL 185160; courtesy of YNPMC.)

The present post exchange, constructed in 1905, gave soldiers a place to play cards, socialize, and relax. This c. 1901 image was taken at its predecessor, the earlier post exchange (see the building on page 51, top left). (02990; courtesy of YNPDSF.)

A soldier's life was not always merely drills. Sometimes it included thrills, such as in this c. 1909 photograph of soldier George Petrach trying out his prowess at riding his horse standing up. (11552; courtesy of YNPDSF.)

Four

BUILDING ROADS IN AMERICA'S FIRST NATIONAL PARK

Road building in Yellowstone began with civilian superintendent P.W. Norris in 1878. Norris used the first congressional money ever allocated, plus some of his own money, to build crude roads that were widely criticized. But his maps make it clear that he established the present Grand Loop Road's general route, and his roads were better than no roads at all.

In 1883, Gen. Philip Sheridan handpicked Lt. Dan Kingman of the US Army Corps of Engineers to begin building roads and bridges in the special place upon which Sheridan kept a special eye. Working until 1887, Kingman "established the park road plan that has proven so satisfactory over the years." He planned a road system that would "enable tourists to visit the principal points of interest . . . without retracing their steps." He recommended and established standards for future roads but, like his successors, discovered that he was often caught up in repairing existing alignments rather creating new roads. Kingman stated that his road plan was submitted with the hope that Yellowstone could be "preserved as nearly . . . as the hand of nature left it." His stability and competence set a high standard for the Army engineers' future road program in the park.

Subsequent engineers were not as visionary as Kingman. Clinton Sears was a short-termer, Charles Allen was a victim of poor congressional funding, and William Craighill was overshadowed by his boss, Maj. W.A. Jones. Jones was a difficult personality whose foibles resulted in the park's road building being returned to superintendents for a little over four years (1894–1899), notwithstanding the fine efforts of an assistant, Hiram M. Chittenden, from 1891 to 1893.

Placed in charge of park road building in 1891, Chittenden's excellent work on the Old Faithful-West Thumb road was handicapped by Major Jones, and Chittenden left the park to launch another career as a historian. He returned between 1899 and 1906, and ultimately became the Yellowstone road engineer who "stands out above all others." Chittenden revamped the Mammoth-Golden Gate road, erected Fishing Bridge and Roosevelt Arch, constructed the Canyon-Tower road, and completely redesigned the village of Mammoth. Six engineers after him were unremarkable, at least in Yellowstone.

Colonel P. W. Norris and Party.

Second superintendent P.W. Norris, second from right, built the first road from Mammoth to Old Faithful, where he posed with his laborers for this photograph on August 30, 1878. Even though he was later criticized for the quality of his roads, Norris did the best he could with a few sharp axes, sturdy shovels, and the calloused hands of a few good men. (YELL 36812; courtesy of YNPMC.)

Lt. Dan Kingman, second from right in the tall boots, was assigned in 1883 by the US Army engineers the monumental task of building a network of permanent roadways in Yellowstone to replace Norris's primitive roads in 1883. (YELL 9110; courtesy of YNPMC.)

The first road built through Golden Gate Canyon (1884–1885) required a lot of man power and expert engineering. These men were part of a crew under Dan Kingman and his foreman, Ed Lamartine. Note the workmen's equipment for the task: shovels. The stone pillar in the center of the photograph was then named the Pillar of Hercules and has remained part of the roadway to this day. (YELL 7676; courtesy of YNPMC.)

According to Kingman's notes on the building of the Golden Gate Bridge, "the canyon wall was nearly vertical and sufficient roadway could be secured only by cutting and breaking down solid rock over 100 feet. The cost of this would have been excessive. The road in this portion was supported by timber trestles." This photograph was taken around 1885. (BS22, photograph AE-19; courtesy of YNPMC.)

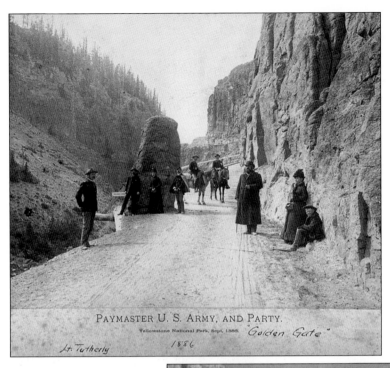

PAYMASTER U. S. ARMY, AND PARTY.
Yellowstone National Park, Sept. 1886. "Golden Gate"
Lt. Tutherly   1886

The route through Golden Gate Canyon as built in 1884–1885 offered horse-drawn coaches and wagons a gentler grade (shown here in 1886) than the older route to the north via Snow Pass, which was very steep. Standing at left is 1st Lt. Herbert Tutherly, and the Army paymaster is at center. George Tutherly is the small boy at right. (Courtesy of YNPMC.)

Pictured in 1907, this stretch of roadway from Rustic Falls to the bridge was dubbed Kingman Pass to honor Lt. Dan Kingman for his monumental task in building this difficult section of roadway. Note the log-and-corduroy construction of Kingman's trestled viaduct that bridged the gap at the upper end of the Golden Gate Canyon. (YELL 10451; courtesy of YNPMC.)

Even though the route through Golden Gate Canyon was better than going over Snow Pass, the stability of the trestle bridge was still questionable. Hence, the posting of signs at both ends of the bridge with the recommendation "Walk Your Horses." (BS22, photograph AE-24; courtesy of YNPMC.)

On his first tour of duty in Yellowstone, US Army engineer Hiram Chittenden, pictured here around 1903, primarily supervised road-building activities from 1891 until 1893. During his second term from 1899 until 1906, Chittenden would not only oversee the completion of the Grand Loop Road around the park but also the construction of several significant bridges, other roadways, and a reservoir. Today's Chittenden Road is named for him. (02970; courtesy of YNPDSF.)

One of Chittenden's tasks in 1900–1901 was to replace Kingman's tenuous wooden trestle roadway in Golden Gate Canyon. His dismantling of the trestle-scaffolding is shown here. (BS22, photograph AE-24; courtesy of YNPMC.)

No small undertaking, constructing a roadway along the vertical stone wall of Golden Gate Canyon required a lot of manpower. This was the second such construction, which occurred in 1900–1901. (BS22, photograph AE-26; courtesy of YNPMC.)

Chittenden's plan to remodel Kingman's causeway through Golden Gate required widening the road, and thus, the Pillar of Hercules had to be moved farther from the cliff. Though the park visitors continued to assume that it was firmly attached to the surrounding rock, it was in fact just an ornamental feature of the bridge. (BS22, photograph AE-32; courtesy of YNPMC.)

The men charged with moving the Pillar of Hercules in 1900–1901 probably felt that their job was as nothing short of a Herculean task. It is possible that Chittenden and his engineers decided to keep the rock in place rather than remove it, because they may have felt it would give visitors a sense of security to see rock on both sides of the road here. (YELL 7923; courtesy of YNPMC.)

Chittenden's sturdier concrete viaduct, pictured around 1901, surely must have given more than one visitor a sense of security as he or she traveled through the canyon. (02915; courtesy of YNPDSF.)

Knowing that they were on a sturdy overpass, stage drivers must have breathed a sigh of relief as they whipped their horses and full coaches through the Golden Gate Canyon and into the park's interior. Chittenden's bridge remained until it was replaced in 1934 and again in 1977. This photograph was taken after 1900. (Courtesy of Bob Berry.)

Chittenden's crew operated from this complex of buildings in Mammoth around 1900. Considering the dressy look of their clothing, one wonders whether this photograph was taken on a Sunday. (BS22, photograph AE-133; courtesy of YNPMC.)

While Superintendent P.W. Norris only had axes and shovels, the Army Corps of Engineers was better supplied with construction equipment, such as seen here sometime after 1900. Beginning in 1901, sprinkler wagons were used to sprinkle park roads to reduce the dust from the numerous, daily coaches and wagons transporting visitors through Yellowstone. (BS22, photograph AE-137; courtesy of YNPMC.)

Yellowstone's terrain and changeable weather constantly made travel through the park a challenge, even with gradually improving roads. (02828; courtesy of YNPDSF.)

The road going over Craig Pass and past Isa Lake crossed the Continental Divide twice before dropping east into the West Thumb area of Yellowstone Lake. Hiram Chittenden supervised this difficult section of road construction, completed in late 1891. (Courtesy of Bob Berry.)

In this 1903 H.C. White stereoview, a two-horse surrey leaves Obsidian Cliff and heads north toward Mammoth Hot Springs over a US Army Corps road and bridge. (Courtesy of Bob Berry.)

Touting the road engineering of Hiram Chittenden, photographer T.W. Ingersoll captioned this 1905 view as "The Magnificent New Virginia Canyon Road and Virginia Falls." Just as today, better roads meant increased speeds, as illustrated by the volume of dust behind the coach in this image. (Courtesy of Bob Berry.)

Travel through Yellowstone on dirt roads was always dusty business. For the first coach, the air quality was not too bad. However, any coach and its passengers that traveled behind another (as in the photograph below) was inescapably covered in a cloud of airborne sand and powdered limestone, as pulverized by narrow, numberless wagon wheels. (BS22, photograph AE-66; courtesy of YNPMC.)

Traveler G.L. Henderson noted in 1885 that "you either ride in your own dust and in that of the carriages behind you, or, if there is a head wind, the dust is driven into your face with a force that blinds and maddens you." (BS22, photograph AE-70; courtesy of YNPMC.)

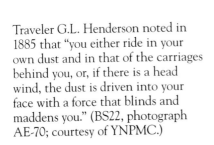

Building roads was only one of the responsibilities for the Army Corps of Engineers. Once the roads were built, members of the Corps were responsible for maintaining them, including road sprinkling with wagons like this one, photographed after 1900. It kept at bay the all-pervasive dust. (02918; courtesy of YNPDSF.)

In 1903, Hiram Chittenden had constructed this ornamental building, later dubbed the Pagoda, as the official office of the US engineer. In the previous year, he had built the tasteful house behind it to serve as his residence. (Lee Whittlesey collection.)

With lots of rivers, creeks, and streams coursing through Yellowstone National Park, bridge building was a constant enterprise for construction workers. An example was this bridge on the west side of Gardner River across from Eagle Nest Rock. (BS22, photograph AE-18; courtesy of YNPMC.)

4519. Eagle Nest Rock, Montana.
Copyright 1901, by George W. Griffith

Completed by 1901, the bridge behind the small girl represented just one of four bridges that had to be constructed over the Gardner River. An older bridge can also be seen here at right. (Courtesy of Bob Berry.)

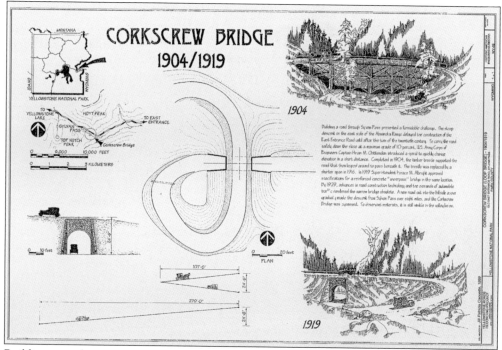

Building a road to open up an entrance to Yellowstone from the east (1901–1905) was probably one of the most formidable challenges that Hiram Chittenden faced. Using his seemingly limitless ingenuity, he designed this unique bridge that looped coaches around one of the steepest sections of road through Sylvan Pass. (Courtesy of Library of Congress.)

Completed in 1905, Chittenden's corkscrew bridge proved to be an inventive and practical way for vehicles to safely ascend or descend the roadway's 10-percent grade, as illustrated by this two-horse surrey. In 1919, the National Park Service redesigned the bridge for automobiles, and remnants of it remain on the site today, below the present road's alignment. (16349; courtesy of YNPDSF.)

4274. Concrete Bridges, Yellowstone Canyon, Yellowstone National Park

This post-1914 H.H. Tammen postcard illustrates the juxtaposition of two of the major bridges that serviced the Grand Canyon of the Yellowstone region in the early 1900s. The Jay Creek Bridge (later called Canyon Bridge) is to the right, and the Melan Arch (later called Chittenden Bridge) is at rear left. (Lee Whittlesey collection.)

The original Jay Creek Bridge was an ornate arched bridge, built between 1893 and 1895. Col. W.A. Jones, the overseer of construction, spared no expense in spending the park's road budget for the entire year on this one project. In 1914, the wooden bridge was replaced by a sturdier concrete bridge, partly in preparation for automobile traffic. (Courtesy of Bob Berry.)

An experienced engineer such as Hiram Chittenden had no trouble looking at this site above the Upper Falls and deeming it suitable for the construction of a bridge to span the mighty Yellowstone River. (BS22, photograph AE-49; courtesy of YNPMC.)

Hiram Chittenden began and completed the concrete bridge in 1903. He named it the Melan Arch bridge after the engineer who designed that style of bridge, but later park managers renamed it in honor of Chittenden. (BS22, photograph 8L-b1; courtesy of YNPMC.)

As construction on the east entrance road progressed, Chittenden built this 360-foot bridge across the Yellowstone River near Lake Outlet in 1902. Although it is considered the original Fishing Bridge, the structure did not receive that name until 1914. (BS22, photograph 11.N.b1; courtesy of YNPMC.)

The water at Fort Yellowstone and Mammoth had always been less than adequate in both supply and quality. Chittenden's answer to this problem involved building a reservoir to collect and store water from Glen Creek, while also using the water to generate electricity. He chose this site near old Camp Sheridan for the reservoir and began its construction in 1901, after he built the road along the base of the Mammoth terraces. This photograph was probably taken in 1900, and the woman at right may be Mrs. Hiram Chittenden. (BS22, photograph AE-189; courtesy of YNPMC.)

Chittenden was a man who got things done and who brought in all the men needed to complete the job. After his crews of workmen with mere shovels and horse-drawn carts dug the entire reservoir by hand, they erected this wood frame (pictured 1900–1901) in preparation for the pouring of concrete for the dam. (BS22, photograph SE-143; courtesy of YNPMC.)

In this c. 1901 photograph, several workmen seem to be doing some last minute smoothing out of the concrete dam, while other men inside the reservoir watch the water flowing in and beginning to fill the reservoir. (BS22, photograph AE-147; courtesy of YNPMC.)

Characteristic of Chittenden's resourcefulness, the fountain in this c. 1901 photograph was not just for show; it had a practical function, as well. The "irrigation fountain" watered the parade grounds and helped grow the lush lawn that continues to grace Mammoth to this day. Note the Fort Yellowstone buildings in the background. (BS22, photograph AE-181; courtesy of YNPMC.)

This photograph affords a panoramic overview of the reservoir with Camp Sheridan in center of the background and P.W. Norris's blockhouse still standing guard on Capitol Hill. In essence, much of the infrastructure that helped to establish Mammoth as the successful touristic place it is today is due to Chittenden and his engineering initiatives. (BS22, photograph AE-178; courtesy of YNPMC.)

Five

OUTPOSTS AND PERILOUS SERVICE

While Fort Yellowstone proper was located at Mammoth Hot Springs, the park's vast interior required the Army to maintain soldier stations at six locations, plus use of "snowshoe cabins" for backcountry patrol. Initially, Captain Harris manned stations at Norris, Soda Butte, Grand Canyon, Riverside (three miles inside the west entrance), Upper Geyser Basin (Old Faithful), Lower Geyser Basin, and later at Yellowstone Lake, Fountain, South Entrance, West Thumb, and Tower. His successor, Capt. Frazier Boutelle, built 16 backcountry cabins for patrol purposes so that the soldiers would have reasonable quarters while watching for illegal hunters (called "poachers"). These soldier stations and cabins were the beginnings of a ranger-station and patrol-cabin system that the National Park Service still uses today.

The duty was sometimes dangerous because of harsh winters, wilderness hazards, and criminals. In 1887, Captain Harris's men made the first arrests for poaching. During the Army's 32 years of duty in Yellowstone, seven soldiers froze to death at their stations or on trips without adequate equipment. Pvt. Andrew Preiber died in 1893 on a one-man, late-night horse ride to Gardiner. David Mathews froze in 1894 on a solo ski trip from Riverside to Gibbon River, and Captain Anderson believed him killed by poachers. Immediately ordered to travel in pairs in winter, John Davis disobeyed orders and skied alone from Lake to West Thumb, where he froze to death at minus 35 degrees. Corp. Christ Martin was killed in an avalanche in 1904 at Snowslide Creek, named for the incident. Lt. Joe McDonald died in 1916 at Mammoth, also in an avalanche. Richard Hurley apparently froze at Snake Station in 1904. Pvt. Presley Vance froze to death at Elk Park after getting drunk and falling off his horse in 1908. Four soldiers drowned in park waters: one in Bath Lake in 1898 while swimming, one in Gardner River in 1910 while drunk, and two in 1918 at Trout Lake while fishing in a defective boat. In 1912, a sergeant at east entrance shot two of his own men in one of the worst cases of "cabin fever" recorded by the Army. And on five occasions, the Army chased bandits who held up park stagecoaches.

The Norris Soldier Station, built in 1908, is shown here as it appeared 1911–1913. It was the third soldier station erected at Norris. Very little is known about the first station, but the second one, which was built in 1897, burned down in 1908. Note the stonework sign in front of the building, which suggests that soldiers of F Troop, First Cavalry were stationed at Norris. (YELL 9746; YNPMC.)

Taken by Jack Haynes in 1917, this image shows two soldiers and the addition of a fence to the dry landscape at Norris Soldier Station. Today, the station serves as the Museum of the National Park Ranger. (BS22, photograph7G-1; courtesy of YNPMC.)

The Canyon Soldier Station was built in 1898. By 1914, when this photograph was taken, it had become very popular to bedeck stations and residences with elk horns, and to use the gnarled wood that grew throughout the park for ornamental railings on bridges and buildings. (11555; courtesy of YNPDSF.)

By 1917, the Canyon Soldier Station had lost most of its decorative elements. The National Park Service took over occupancy of this station, pictured in 1917, as well as all of the soldier stations and converted them into ranger stations between 1916 and 1918. (BC22, photograph 228L-7; courtesy of YNPMC.)

The Fountain Soldier Station, built in 1887, held five men. It was located northeast of where Fountain Flats Drive begins today, and the small building at right (known as the "doghouse") was where visiting officers were lodged. Soldiers from this station helped Firehole Hotel winter-keeper E.C. Culver bury his wife, Mattie Culver, after she died from tuberculosis in the winter of 1889. Her grave remains at Nez Perce Picnic area. (BS22, photograph11-E1; courtesy of YNPMC.)

After the completion of the final section of the Grand Loop Road from Old Faithful to West Thumb in late 1891, the Army established an outpost at West Thumb. This soldier station was constructed later—in 1904. Note the Sibley tent at the side for accommodating extra soldiers during the busy summer tourist season. The building at far right is unidentified but may have been the West Thumb Lunch Station. (10644; courtesy of YNPDSF.)

The building that predated the Lake Soldier Station was erected in 1884 under the purview of the civilian administrators, and the Army took possession of it in 1887 to house soldiers patrolling the Yellowstone Lake area. This photograph was taken around 1900, following the construction of a new soldier station in 1898. (Courtesy of YNPMC.)

By 1917, when park photographer Jack Haynes took this photograph, the Lake Soldier Station had acquired a few more elk-antler racks and was nicely enclosed by a log-rail fence. (BS22, photograph 12M-3; courtesy of YNPMC.)

The Snake River Soldier Station near south entrance was built to help protect the south boundary of Yellowstone and the Timberland Reserve (part of today's area between Yellowstone and Grand Teton Parks within and outside of the John D. Rockefeller Memorial Parkway). This is how it appeared in 1917. (BS22, photograph 21H-1; courtesy of YNPMC.)

Located just west of Calcite Springs overlook, this was the original Tower Fall Soldier Station, as it appeared about 1905. In 1907, a new station was built near Tower Junction following the erection of the Wylie Permanent Camping Company's "Roosevelt Camp" nearby. (11555; courtesy of YNPDSF.)

In this 1905 photograph, the Tower Fall soldier station was adorned with a few more antlers on its rooftop as well as attracting the real article. Elk like this one were sometimes the only company these soldiers received, because Tower Fall was not on the general tourist route. (Courtesy of Milwaukee Public Library.)

In 1914, Yellowstone experienced its fourth recorded stagecoach robbery. In this dramatic snapshot, the highwayman, Edward B. Trafton, was photographed sorting his loot after holding up 15 stagecoaches. Both soldiers and civilian scouts were alerted and began to track him. He was eventually arrested by federal agents and served five years in Leavenworth. (Courtesy of YNPMC.)

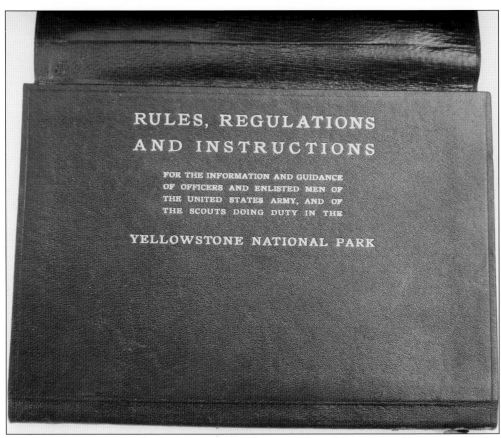

Upon assignment to Fort Yellowstone, each soldier was issued his personal volume of *Rules, Regulations and Instructions*, in what became commonly known as the "little red book," published in 1907. Many of the copies in the park library remain curved in shape from years of being carried in soldiers' back pockets. (Lee Whittlesey collection.)

KILLING COYOTES, ETC.

10. Scouts and noncommissioned officers in charge of stations throughout the park are authorized and directed to kill mountain lions, coyotes, and timber wolves. They will do this themselves, and will not delegate the authority to anyone else. They will report at the end of each month, in writing, the number of such animals killed, and will retain all skins or scalps in their personal possession until directed what to do with them.

While soldiers and scouts were commanded to protect the "good animals," like elk, deer, and antelope, they were ordered to kill the "bad animals," such as wolves, coyotes, and mountain lions. The philosophy of protecting all animals, including predators, had not yet evolved. The passage above is from the "little red book." (Lee Whittlesey collection.)

At the Soda Butte Ranger Station in the Lamar Valley area in the northeast region of the park, soldiers in this undated photograph proudly displayed their catch of the day, a coyote skin, around 1907. The Lamar Valley area was heavily patrolled by soldiers during the winter months due to excessive incidents of poaching there. (16219; courtesy of YNPMC.)

Cush Jones (shown here), brother of the park's well-known Buffalo Jones, took seriously his orders to kill coyotes, wolves, and mountain lions and displayed his hunting skills by lining his walls with trophy pelts. (16218; courtesy of YNPDSF.)

In this 1913 real-photo postcard, an unidentified man walks to the Upper Geyser Basin Soldier Station at Old Faithful. Note the Sibley tents that were set up to house extra troops during the heavy tourist season. (Courtesy of Bob Berry.)

This c. 1904 image of the Old Faithful Station shows the barn at rear, outhouse in center, and storage shed at bottom. Then located in the oxbow on Firehole River about one-quarter mile north of Old Faithful Inn, this complex originally served civilian superintendents, between 1879 and 1885. Taken over by the Army in 1886, it was gradually added to until torn down by the NPS in 1921. (02892; courtesy of YNPDSF.)

This c. 1902 view of the Old Faithful Soldier Station shows only three buildings, which almost seem to be invisible in the dreamy, vaporized world of the Upper Geyser Basin. The first building at Old Faithful was constructed by Yellowstone's second superintendent, P.W. Norris, in 1879. He described the building as "an earth-roofed, loop-holed log house with a good stone chimney and located between the Castle and the Beehive Geysers." Norris's building, located near the Firehole River, was probably the foundational structure for the Army's soldier station complex, which was erected at the same location. Exactly when the Army built these structures is unknown. The Army added buildings to the complex until 1916, and in 1916–1917, the National Park Service took over the buildings and used them as the first Old Faithful ranger station until a new ranger station was constructed southwest of the Old Faithful Lodge in 1921. (Courtesy of Library of Congress.)

No trip will be made on snowshoes by less than two men. If he party is not conducted by a duly authorized scout, it should be led by the most experienced soldier. Wise precaution must be exercised to prevent separation of the party.

WINTER PATROLLING.

The noncommissioned officer in charge of the station must see that the men going out on a snowshoe trip are properly clothed and equipped. Heavy winter underclothing must be worn; also German socks and overshoes, a cap with visor and flaps to protect the head and ears, and suitable warm covering for the hands. The feet must be kept dry and clean. Matches, a good axe, and sufficient food to provide against accidents must always be carried. Colored glasses to prevent snow blindness are necessary, and the frames should be wound with woolen yarn to prevent freezing the face. The map and compass should always be carried.

Snowshoeing is not dangerous work if proper precautions are taken, but judgment and caution are necessary. The use of intoxicants or stimulants, even in the slightest degree, is dangerous while on a snowshoe trip.

During the winter duty period, patrolling and scouting will be constantly carried on, and when camps are made they will, if possible, be selected so as to be hidden from poachers who may be in the park. Patrols and scouts will avoid the regular trails as far as possible, and will vary their different trips as much as the character of the country will allow.

The soldiers' "little red book" also gave explicit instructions on winter patrolling, including clothing to be worn and items to be carried—colored glasses wrapped in yarn to prevent them from freezing to one's face, matches, axe, compass, and map. Yellowstone's winters were not to be taken lightly, and after some learning experiences involving fatalities, the Army became very strict in its winter policies. (Lee Whittlesey collection.)

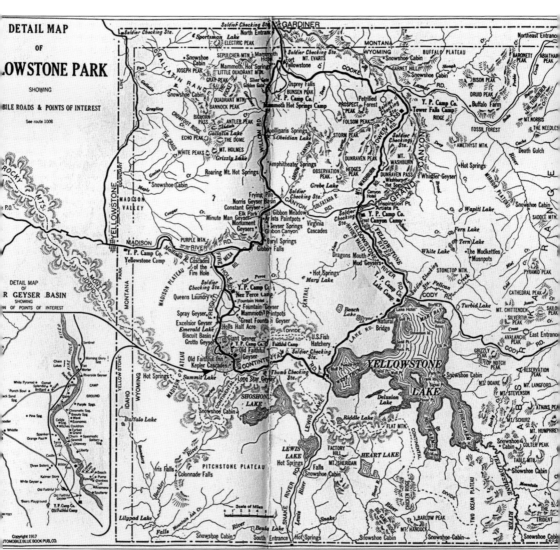

The first six Army "snowshoe cabins" used for sheltering soldiers and civilian scouts charged with patrolling Yellowstone's remote backcountry and pursuing poachers were built around 1890. The cabins were described by Captain Bradley in his 1900 *Proceedings of the Association of Military Surgeons* article, titled "The Ski and Its Use for Military Purposes in Yellowstone National Park," as "little huts" that were "about a day's trip apart." His article also made clear that the cabins were very rudimentary with a rough fireplaces for warmth and only containing only bare necessities, such as "a small amount of food, some bedding, fuel, cooking utensils, an axe, and a shovel." By 1900, there were 19 snowshoe cabins dotting Yellowstone's backcountry. This 1917 Automobile Blue Book map is one of the rare maps that identifies the various snowshoe cabins and their locations. (Elizabeth Watry collection.)

This gent's ski apparel certainly looks warm, but probably would only be practical for skiing around Mammoth. The heavy wool coat would weigh down a soldier trying to do some distance in the snow. (YELL 482; courtesy of YNPMC.)

The long skis that the soldiers used were called Norwegian Snowshoes. They typically were nine feet long and weighed around 10 pounds. Photographed sometime between 1886 and 1900, these men at Golden Gate Bridge may have been returning from a patrol of the Swan Lake area. Strong canyon winds here routinely kept the road free of snow, while just above these men snow often drifted to 10 feet deep. (YELL 9369; courtesy of YNPMC.)

Yellowstone's winter ski patrols became legendary, because they tested the mettle of even the hardiest men. Note here the skiers' use of only one pole. On downhill slopes, the pole could be put between the skiers' legs, which would allow them to control the rate of descent as they essentially rode the pole. The soldiers shown here in 1894 made the arrest of poacher Ed Howell. (YELL 36998; courtesy of YNPMC.)

Forest and Stream reporter Emerson Hough captured in 1894 the extreme conditions that soldiers and scouts faced when he opined, "I never knew . . . I had seen the Park . . . in all its . . . forbidding . . . until I . . . traversed with weary feet some of those endless miles of bottomless snow." The mixture of Army uniforms here—with one man wearing "blues" and everyone else wearing khaki—dates the photograph to the color-change era of 1902–1904. (YELL 44519; courtesy of YNPMC.)

This photograph of a snowshoe cabin is one of the rare winter images of those primitive winter outposts. Its location has been the subject of debate for decades. The most plausible suggestions include "Mud Volcano" and upper Alum Creek. (YELL 127395; courtesy of YNPMC.)

A TRAGEDY OF THE TRAIL: BRINGING A DEAD SOLDIER IN ON HIS SKI.

After several men froze to death, Capt. George Anderson ordered all snowshoe patrols to travel in pairs. In December 1897, W.H. Davis and a partner started out on snowshoes traveling from Lake to West Thumb. While his companion turned back after 10 miles, Davis did not and died. Finding Davis frozen, soldiers dragged him back to Mammoth on one of his own skis. The story was reported in *National Magazine*. (YELL 125346; courtesy of YNPMC.)

Morrison   *Stitham*   *Holte*   *Lieut. Lindsl*

Trip to Fall river 189

A ski trip to Fall River was rigorous in winter. Here, a group plows through the southwest corner of the park in search of poachers in 1897–1898. Skiers here are identified in handwriting as, from left to right, scout James Morrison, Private Stitham, Pvt. Peter Holte, and Lt. Elmer Lindsley. They patrolled from Snake River Soldier Station, January 16–27, 1898, as reported by Lindsley in Yellowstone archive document 4877. (YELL 951; courtesy of YNPMC.)

These soldiers are probably preparing to depart on a ski patrol near the east entrance, one of the more dangerous locations due to threat of avalanches, hence a group of five for safety. (160-86P; Courtesy of Park County, Wyoming, Archives.)

In early 1887, Frank Haynes took this image as Canyon winter keepers and some of Haynes's party members shoveled snow from the first Canyon Hotel. Then as now, snowfall in the Canyon area was recorded in feet, rather than in inches. The snow accumulation on the roofs was so deep that it sometimes had to be cut in blocks to remove it and eliminate the danger of collapse from the weight. (YELL 951; courtesy of YNPMC.)

This soldier appears to have been checking on the buildings at one of the Wylie Permanent Camping Company camps during the period 1906–1916. While the accommodation tents were dismantled each season, the roofs of the more permanent structures, such as kitchens, were subject to collapse from the weight of Yellowstone's heavy snowfall. (Courtesy of Bob Berry.)

Six

A PRESIDENTIAL VISIT

Presidents visited Yellowstone National Park before and after the US Army's administration, but only Pres. Theodore Roosevelt elected to visit the park during the Army's actual occupation.

Roosevelt's visit occurred in April 1903. It was a personal vacation for him that turned out to be timely for Yellowstone, because observers were then proclaiming that the park's north entrance needed not only a fancier entryway but also an appropriate depot for its newly extended railway. When Roosevelt announced that he intended to visit the park, citizens of Gardiner and Mammoth decided to ask him to lay the cornerstone at the proposed new entryway and simultaneously welcome the Northern Pacific Railroad to Yellowstone.

The US Army was immediately involved in this trip, which became Roosevelt's longest, most-intense immersion in the wonders of Yellowstone. Acting superintendent Maj. John Pitcher met Roosevelt's train at Cinnabar, Montana, on April 8 and served as his escort for the next 16 days.

Accompanied by C Troop, Major Pitcher took Roosevelt and naturalist John Burroughs to Mammoth for the night, and the next morning, they began their trip into the park. Billy Hofer served as guide, with the soldiers of B Troop as protection, because Roosevelt had given orders that he was not to be disturbed. For the next two weeks, he tramped, rode, and skied his way through some of Yellowstone's most beautiful country, savoring wildlife, soaking up Western scenery, and enjoying the stories of Burroughs, Hofer, and Pitcher while telling a few himself. In camp near Pleasant Valley, Army engineer Hiram Chittenden presented Roosevelt with a citizens' letter asking him to dedicate the new entrance at Gardiner, and the president accepted.

On April 24, amidst extra trains and 40 extra Livingston stagecoaches along with a band and massive decorations in the town of Gardiner, some 3,700 visitors, citizens, and Masons welcomed Roosevelt. He gave a rousing speech, mortared the cornerstone into place, and posed for many photographs before riding to his waiting train at Cinnabar. He never again visited Yellowstone, so he never passed through the Roosevelt Arch built on the site that today bears his name.

President Roosevelt arrived at the Northern Pacific railway terminus in Cinnabar, Montana, on April 8, 1903. He was greeted by Yellowstone's acting superintendent, Maj. John Pitcher, at far right. According to the *Livingston Enterprise* newspaper, Roosevelt said, "My dear Major, I am back in my own country again." The two had met years earlier in Yellowstone when Pitcher was ranked lower and Roosevelt was hunting outside the park. (Courtesy of Calisphere.edu.)

Roosevelt laughed heartily on numerous occasions, as he surely enjoyed being back in his beloved West and in his favorite seat, a saddle. According to photographic record at the Yellowstone Gateway Museum, the grey horse named Bonaparte that Roosevelt was riding here was his faithful steed during the entire trip, probably chosen because it was docile and not likely to throw the president. (Courtesy of Bob Berry.)

Maj. John Picher (at far left), naturalist John Burroughs (the white bearded man), and William Loeb (presiding secretary) joined Roosevelt for a photograph taken on the porch of present NPS building no. 5 at Fort Yellowstone. It is believed that this is where T.R. stayed for his first night in the park. Others are probably Mrs. Pitcher, a Secret Service man, and Harry Child, park concessioner. (Courtesy of Bob Berry.)

President Roosevelt and the noted naturalist John Burroughs, at Fort Yellowstone, Yellowstone Park. Copyright 1903 by Underwood & Underwood.

President Roosevelt at Fort Yellowstone, ready for his trip through Yellowstone Park. Copyright 1903 by Underwood & Underwood

On the morning after his arrival in Yellowstone, Roosevelt mounted up to embark on a two-week camping trip into the interior of the park. (Courtesy of Bob Berry.)

Roosevelt and acting superintendent Maj. John Pitcher were old friends with some of the same interests. They both were devotees of outdoor life, which included being expert marksmen and accomplished horsemen. Here, they were shown on the Mammoth terraces. (02968; courtesy of YNPDSF.)

This was one of camps set up for Roosevelt's tour in the park. While the location is not identified on the photograph, the topography suggests the camp was in the northeastern portion of the park. (02967; courtesy of YNPDSF.)

Major Pitcher and John Burroughs (sitting on a seat fashioned out of an elk antler and a buffalo robe) were captured here as they relaxed in camp. Burroughs later wrote a book that was partly about the trip, titled *Camping and Tramping with Roosevelt*. (14514; courtesy of YNPDSF.)

Famed Yellowstone guide Elwood "Uncle Billy" Hofer (seated at far right) served as the continuing guide for Roosevelt's Yellowstone excursion. (Courtesy of Library of Congress.)

To protect the president of the United States, the Army sent a force of cavalry to stand guard while Roosevelt enjoyed the backcountry of Yellowstone. Roosevelt's own Secret Service men, shown in other photographs, seem to have remained with his train at Cinnabar while soldiers accompanied the president. (14509; courtesy of YNPDSF.)

Pictured in 1903, this unidentified, straight-faced, armed soldier standing at attention apparently took his duty to protect the president very seriously. (09193; courtesy of YNPDSF.)

For some soldiers, such as this young man, being assigned to protect the president was an honor that was probably not equaled in their lifetime and that probably remained a treasured event and memory. (14512; courtesy of YNPDSF.)

THE PRESIDENT, MR. BURROUGHS AND "BILLY" HOFER ON THE TRAIL FROM HELL ROARING TO STERN CREEK.

This image, which appeared in a 1903 *Illustrated Sporting News* article about Roosevelt's visit to Yellowstone, revealed a rare moment of the president enjoying the solitude of the backcountry with Burroughs and Hofer and without being surrounded by Secret Service men. However, the soldiers who protected him were probably not far behind. (Courtesy of *Illustrated Sporting News*.)

Roosevelt's backcountry attire during his Yellowstone trip seemed to match his penchant for living the "strenuous life." This 1903 photograph was taken by Wilbur Hunt, surveyor for the US Army Corps of Engineers. (02969; courtesy of YNPDSF.)

Roosevelt's trip to Yellowstone coincided with the establishment of the north entrance arch at Gardiner, Montana. Plans for the celebration being underway, the suggestion arose to have Roosevelt dedicate the arch's cornerstone. Here, mounted cavalrymen proceeded to the ceremony on April 24. They were wearing blue uniforms, although the Army changed to khakis in 1902. The stereoview caption read, "Fort Yellowstone Cavalry—the U.S. Soldiers who guard the great National Park." (Courtesy of Bob Berry.)

One of Roosevelt's requests was that the public be allowed to assemble close to the podium for his speech. From the looks of the gathering crowd, that request was fulfilled. According to historian Aubrey Haines, four special trains had been run from Livingston to Gardiner that day so that the local populace could attend the ceremony. One newspaper's estimate of the crowd size was 3,700. (Courtesy of Calisphere.edu.)

The Masons, wearing their signature white aprons, began their procession on Gardiner's main street, presumably Park Street, and marched to the arch location at the west edge of town. The man at the front of the line holding the trowel with which Roosevelt would mortar the cornerstone was probably Gardiner's "mayor," James McCartney. (Courtesy of Calisphere.edu.)

Ceremonies began at 4:00 p.m., with Roosevelt preparing the cornerstone's seat with mortar and trowel. Army engineer Hiram Chittenden stands profile at center in billed hat while uniformed Maj. John Pitcher is at bottom of photograph, also wearing a billed hat with his back to the camera. Roosevelt, hatless and located two persons left and one person up from Pitcher, awaits the cornerstone. (Courtesy of Calisphere.edu.)

Here, Theodore Roosevelt addresses the crowd from the decorated platform at Gardiner, his notes probably in his left hand. Hiram Chittenden stands to the right in khaki uniform. From left to right are four sitting Masonic dignitaries, acting superintendent Maj. John Pitcher in khaki uniform, unidentified (perhaps hotel concessioner Harry Child), John Burroughs (white beard), James McCartney ("mayor" of Gardiner), and William Loeb (presidential secretary in top hat). (Courtesy of YNPMC.)

Seven

"As a Consequence of Their Good Work"

As a result of 32 years of Army administration, Yellowstone was protected where earlier it had been threatened. "Not one of the notable geyser formations," wrote Captain Harris in 1886, "has escaped mutilation." Tourists' hacking off pieces of geysers, driving logs into spring-holes, and writing their names on formations had to be stopped, so soldiers marched offenders to the sites of desecrations to scrub out names and strictly guarded the locations to prevent souvenir collecting and vandalism.

In general, soldiers enforced all park rules and regulations, prevented and extinguished forest fires, protected travelers from abuse or extortion by stage drivers and innkeepers, and preserved respect for law and order, not hesitating to "make arrests when necessary." They were instructed to "conduct themselves in a courteous and polite but firm and decided manner."

During the years before 1894, when the Lacey Act went into effect to protect park animals, soldiers dealt with illegal hunters in a specific, extra-legal fashion. They marched the violator to the park boundary and deposited his horse and equipment there. They marched the violator to the opposite park boundary and left him there. He was then not allowed to travel through the park to retrieve his outfit but instead had to travel around the park—often a distance of over 100 miles. This expulsion sometimes followed imprisonment in the guardhouse for up to six weeks before "word" could be "received" that he was being held illegally. The Lacey Act brought statutory law to the park along with a US judge who possessed jurisdiction to prosecute poaching and vandalism.

Beginning in 1907, soldiers carried the "little red book" in their hip pockets that contained the park's organic act, the Lacey Act, the park rules and regulations, and instructions for patrolling. Regulations extended to thermal formations, stock grazing, tree-cutting, hay-cutting, fires, hunting, trapping, fishing, residing in park, guiding, saloons, and private notices.

So, how have historians rated the US Army in Yellowstone? Most agree that it was effective and efficient in its administration, if occasionally overzealous and extralegal. But this was arguably reasonable, given a remote, wilderness environment that truly deserved special protection.

Edward Burton McDowell shot this photograph of a soldier, tourists, and Sponge Geyser with a Kodak round-view camera in 1890. Round-view cameras were short-lived, lasting only from 1888 through 1891, and thus images such as this one are uncommon. (Courtesy of YNPMC.)

The Devils Inkpot in this 1904 Keystone stereoview is being watched by a mounted soldier from a safe distance, as he most likely knew the danger of hot springs and may not have wanted to personally experience any part of a thermal feature named after a fiendish character. Today, this feature at Norris Geyser Basin is called Bathtub Spring. (Courtesy of Library of Congress.)

13589—A Commotion in the Devil's Ink Pot—A Moment of Eruption, Yellowstone National Park, Wyo., U.S.A.

In 1910, these tourists climbed to the top of White Elephant Back Terrace in the upper terrace region of Mammoth Hot Springs, under the guidance of a soldier familiar with the formation's unusual and fragile areas. (Photograph by Florence Streb Fassler; courtesy of Lee Whittlesey collection.)

Posing with pretty women to have their pictures taken was probably one of the more idyllic duties for Army soldiers, as depicted in this real-photo postcard around 1904. The location is Admiration Point overlooking the Main Terrace at Mammoth Hot Springs. (Courtesy of Bob Berry.)

Author Frances Benjamin Johnson captured this soldier enveloped in vapor at Punch Bowl Spring in the Upper Geyser Basin during her trip in 1903. (Courtesy of Library of Congress.)

This statuesque soldier guards a formation known as Pulpit Terrace at Mammoth Hot Springs, sometime between 1904 and 1918. In early days, the terrace was a popular place for visitors to pose for photographs as they pretended to deliver sermons from its "pulpits." (Courtesy of Bob Berry.)

This 1912 Stereo-Travel Company image (probably taken in 1911) captured the panoramic duty station of this lone soldier as he guarded the Main and Jupiter terraces of Mammoth Hot Springs. (Courtesy of Bob Berry.)

Because the eruption of geysers and hot springs was something of a mystery, any inactivity generally brought onlookers closer than what was safe, as depicted by this curious soldier's proximity to Tardy Geyser's opening, probably in 1911. Today, visitors are not allowed to get this close to any geyser, both to protect its fragile crust from destruction and to prevent personal injury. (Courtesy of Bob Berry.)

28. A quiescent and an active Geyser, Upper Basin, Y. N. P. Copyright 1912 by Stereo Travel Co.

Occasionally, soldiers and officers, like anyone else, would sit and enjoy the ambiance of Yellowstone's many rivers, creeks, and springs, as this military man did one day on the Gardner River at "Split Rock" (near Eagle Nest Rock), probably in 1911. (Courtesy of Bob Berry.)

86. Eagle Rock below Mammoth, Y. N. P.
Copyright, 1912, by Stereo Travel Co.

Probably photographed in 1911, a soldier here seems to be reading a letter or perhaps a park guidebook to get information, as Sawmill Geyser playfully erupts behind him. (Courtesy of Bob Berry.)

29. The Sawmill Geyser in action, Upper Basin, Y. N. P.
Copyright, 1912, by Stereo Travel Co.

Army soldiers stand guard atop "the great boiling springs on the Jupiter Terrace," probably in 1903, in this H.C. White Company stereoview. Just over the terrace and below is the location of the Army's original residence, Camp Sheridan. (Courtesy of Bob Berry.)

88. The Hoodoos, on road Mammoth to Norris Basin, Y. N. P.
Copyright, 1912, by Stereo Travel Co.

STEREO-TRAVEL CO.
CORONA, NEW YORK CITY

This soldier standing on top of a piece of fallen travertine, probably in 1911, was dwarfed by the gigantic slabs of travertine in the Hoodoos just south of Mammoth Hot Springs. (Courtesy of Bob Berry.)

Soldiers were also charged with keeping visitors safe, especially as they toured around the geyser basin on mere wood planks that served as early boardwalks. Stepping off of the boardwalks in geyser basin areas then just as now could result in severe burns or even death. Here, a soldier was photographed with a tourist party at Norris Geyser Basin, probably in 1911. (Courtesy of Bob Berry.)

STEREO-TRAVEL CO.
CORONA, NEW YORK CITY

96. Looking toward Black Growler, Norris Basin, Y. N. P.
Copyright, 1912, by Stereo Travel Co.

NORTHERN PACIFIC SCENERY.
F. JAY HAYNES, PUBLISHER, FARGO, D. T.

4548   MAMMOTH PAINT POTS

The two soldiers standing guard over the "Mammoth Paint Pots," today's Fountain Paint Pot, are barely visible at upper center, as the massiveness of the mud pot seems to overwhelm them in this c. 1889 Haynes stereoview. (Courtesy of Bob Berry.)

This rare, c. 1888 T.W. Ingersoll stereoview depicts two soldiers watching over a little-known spring then called "Saphire Spring" in the Upper Geyser Basin. Today, it is called Blue Star Spring. (Courtesy of Bob Berry.)

PHOTOGRAPHED BY T. W. INGERSOLL, ST. PAUL.

1210. B. SAPHIRE SPRING. U.G.B.
YELLOWSTONE NATIONAL PARK.

PHOTOGRAPHED BY T. W. INGERSOLL, ST. PAUL, MINN.

1248 B. BEEHIVE GEYSER CONE.
YELLOWSTONE NATIONAL PARK.

While the activity of Beehive Geyser varied from long periods of dormancy to phases of near daily eruptions, it was a popular geyser for visitors in the Upper Geyser Basin. From the water surrounding the cone in this c. 1888 Ingersoll stereoview, it appears that Beehive had recently erupted or was getting ready to erupt, hence the arrival of the two military sentinels to check it out. (Courtesy of Bob Berry.)

115

Standing atop Jupiter Terrace, a soldier seems to be observing the activity of one of the terraces' many dynamic pools. Bunsen Peak is at rear in this c. 1903 stereoview. (Courtesy of Bob Berry.)

According to the caption of this Stereo-Travel image probably taken in 1911, Hymen Terrace was the "most beautiful of Mammoth Hot Springs Terraces." By that time, the figure of a solitary soldier guard safeguarding formations and thermal features had become a common sight throughout the park. (Courtesy of Bob Berry.)

79. Hymen Terraces, most beautiful of Mammoth Hot Springs Terraces, Y. N. P. Copyright, 1912, by Stereo-Travel Co.

STEREO-TRAVEL CO.
CORONA, NEW YORK CITY.

Upon occasion, military personnel stationed in various geyser basins and points of interest served as interpreters for park visitors. Here, a soldier at far right seems to be explaining the mysteries of Giant Geyser to a group of tourists in or about 1909. Soldiers occasionally did interpretation, but more often their function was protection. (S.D. Butcher and Son; courtesy of Library of Congress.)

no. 2090. Giant Geyser Y.N.P.
Copyrighted by S.D. Butcher & Son 09.

Thermal features were not the only natural wonders protected by the Army. In 1907, the Army erected an iron fence near Tower Junction to protect this petrified tree, because a nearby petrified tree had been completely dismantled by souvenir hunters. (P02-93; courtesy of Park County, Wyoming, Archives.)

In addition to protecting the geological wonders of Yellowstone, the Army was charged with protecting the wildlife. In the winter of 1893–1894, F.J. Haynes photographed these bull elk trudging through the snow. This image is reflective of how vulnerable the animals were during the winter and how they thus could become easy prey for poachers. (10649; courtesy of YNPDSF.)

Apparently, this bull elk became so accustomed to the soldiers' presence that he felt perfectly comfortable lounging in front of the Tower Soldier Station, probably in 1905. (41804; courtesy of Milwaukee Public Library.)

In 1894, Edgar Howell poached bison in Pelican Valley. Skiing there, scout Felix Burgess and Sergeant Troike heard shots. They discovered Howell standing over dead bison and arrested him. Hand labeling identifies the men: Capt. G.L. Scott, Lieutenant Forsyth, scout Burgess, Howell's dog, and Edgar Howell. Burgess's "capture of the dangerous poacher Ed Howell," says historian Haines, "brought him a citation . . . and the thanks of the Boone and Crockett Club." (YELL 1659; courtesy of YNPMC.)

Officers displayed bison heads from poacher Howell to proclaim that protection for park bison was needed. From left to right are Dr. Charles M. Gandy, Lt. John T. Nance, Capt. George L. Scott, and Lieutenant Forsyth. Howell's arrest made national news, resulting in the Lacey Act (1894), which gave the Army legal authority to enforce hunting regulations. At bottom, someone wrote the ominous notation: "Poachers waiting to be shot. Sic simper." (16058; courtesy of YNPDSF.)

As a result of the Lacey Act, Judge John W. Meldrum was assigned to be the US commissioner (judge) in Yellowstone National Park in 1894. His duty as commissioner in the park was unique, as he presided over an area where federal law was the superseding law rather than state law, but he had some state jurisdiction and enforced some state laws. (YELL 7295; courtesy of YNPMC.)

Referred to as the "Grand Old Man of Yellowstone," a moniker he wore well, Judge Meldrum attended to the legal affairs of Yellowstone until his retirement in 1935 at the age of 92. (YELL 7526; courtesy of YNPMC.)

Judge Meldrum probably used this stamp to seal his rulings as well as to sign his correspondence throughout his tenure as Yellowstone's longest serving commissioner. (Lee Whittlesey collection.)

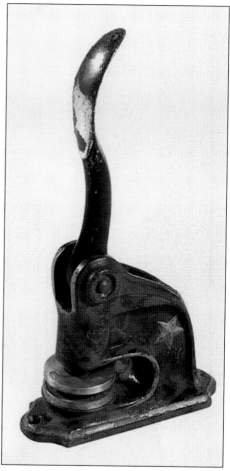

This imprint affirmed Judge Meldrum's official capacity as US commissioner for over 40 years. (Lee Whittlesey collection.)

The soldier standing guard at one of the walking portals of the grand Roosevelt Arch at Yellowstone's north entrance was here nearly obscured by both the massive stone monument that welcomed thousands of visitors and the large-scale landscape that surrounded it in this Forsyth stereoview. (Courtesy of Bob Berry.)

Even though it was a federal preserve, Yellowstone was the scene of five stagecoach holdups during the period 1887–1915. Consequently, soldiers were frequently assigned to escort coaches through previously known robbery areas, such as this route to Mammoth through Gardner Canyon, pictured before 1904. (Courtesy of YNPMC.)

For many first-time travelers to the West, viewing a mounted cavalryman charged with ensuring their safety must have been a comforting sight as they left the civilization of Mammoth Hot Springs and embarked on an adventure into the wilderness of America's Wonderland. This photograph was taken in 1909. (Butcher and Son; courtesy of Bob Berry.)

When the national need arose, the troops assigned to Yellowstone were called to serve in distant locations. Here, soldiers were photographed leaving the park for one of those assignments, probably the Pacific during the Philippine-American War (1899–1902) or Cuba during the Spanish-American War (1898). (Courtesy of Bill Arnold.)

With the flag flying high, the Army rode through Mammoth Hot Springs to answer the call of duty probably in the Philippines around 1900. Note the wooden sidewalks that graced the fort's thoroughfare. (11553; courtesy of YNPDSF.)

To show their patriotic support for the Army, the citizens of Mammoth gathered on the wooden sidewalk of Mammoth Hot Springs's Officers' Row to wave and wish the soldiers farewell. Here, soldiers were riding south past Capitol Hill to descend the park's main road to the railroad station at Gardiner, Montana. (Courtesy of Bill Arnold.)

The commanding presence of Fort Yellowstone in Mammoth Hot Springs was as much an attraction for visitors in search of memorabilia as the colossal National Hotel, as this 1905 postcard attests. (Elizabeth Watry collection.)

Col. Lloyd Milton Brett—Yellowstone's last military superintendent—accompanied the crew of this "Pathfinder" automobile in 1911 as they assessed the practicality of a motorcar route to the park. The Minnesota Automobile Association, which sponsored the survey to help develop tourist routes from St. Paul to the park, eventually improved a primitive road to the park boundary called the Yellowstone Trail. Automobiles driven by the public were formally admitted into Yellowstone in 1915. (Courtesy of YNPMC.)

After signaling the end of the day in Yellowstone for nearly 30 years from the top of Capitol Hill, the sunset cannon was fired for what is believed to have been the last time in 1916. Symbolically, this event signaled the end of the military control of Yellowstone as the Army transferred management of the park to the newly created National Park Service that year. However, due to the shortsighted maneuverings of two Montana congressmen, who cut off congressional funding to the new National Park Service, the Army remained in the park until 1918. The Army left behind an immeasurable legacy of policies and procedures that served to protect and preserve the flora and fauna as well as the natural wonders of Yellowstone. Many of those policies and practices are still in use today. Upon the Army's departure, many of Yellowstone's dedicated soldiers opted to join the National Park Service and thus continued to use their intimate knowledge of the park to safeguard America's Wonderland. (YELL 36929; courtesy of YNPMC.)

BIBLIOGRAPHY

Baldwin, Kenneth H. *Enchanted Enclosure: The Army Engineers and Yellowstone National Park: A Documentary History*. Washington, DC: US Government Printing Office, 1976.

Battle, David G. and Erwin N. Thompson. *Fort Yellowstone: Historic Structures Report*. Denver, CO: Historic Preservation Denver Service Center, 1972.

Chittenden, Hiram. *The Yellowstone National Park: Historical and Descriptive*, 2nd rev. ed. Cincinnati, OH: Stewart & Kidd Company, 1915.

Freeman, Lewis R. *Down the Yellowstone*. New York: Dodd, Mead and Company, 1922.

Haines, Aubrey L. *The Yellowstone Story: A History of Our First National Park*, Vol. 2. Niwot: CO: University of Colorado, 1996.

Hamilton, James M. *History of Yellowstone National Park (Previous to 1895)*. Unpublished manuscript. Yellowstone National Park Library.

Hampton, H. Duane. *How the US Cavalry Saved Our National Parks*. Bloomington, IN: University of Indiana, 1971.

Jacoby, Karl. *Crimes against Nature: Squatters, Poachers, Thieves, and the Hidden History of American Conservation*. Berkeley, CA: University of California Press, 2001.

Remington, Frederick. *Pony Tracks*. Norman, OK: University of Oklahoma, 1961.

Rydell, Kiki and Mary Shivers Culpin. *Managing the "Matchless Wonders:" A History of Administrative Development in Yellowstone National Park, 1872–1965*. Yellowstone National Park, WY: Yellowstone Center for Resources, 2006.

Schullery, Paul. *Yellowstone Ski Pioneers: Peril and Heroism on the Winter Trail*. Worland, WY: High Plains Publishing Company, 1995.

Whittlesey, Lee H. *Death in Yellowstone: Accidents and Foolhardiness in the First National Park*. Boulder, CO: Roberts Rinehart Publishers, 1995.

Whittlesey, Lee H. with Marsha Karle, ed. *A Yellowstone Album: A Photographic Celebration of the First National Park*. Boulder, CO: Roberts Rinehart Publishers, 1997.

Whittlesey, Lee H. "This Modern Saratoga of the Wilderness!": A History of Mammoth Hot Springs and the Village of Mammoth in Yellowstone National Park. National Park Service, in press: 2012.

DISCOVER THOUSANDS OF LOCAL HISTORY BOOKS
FEATURING MILLIONS OF VINTAGE IMAGES

Arcadia Publishing, the leading local history publisher in the United States, is committed to making history accessible and meaningful through publishing books that celebrate and preserve the heritage of America's people and places.

Find more books like this at
www.arcadiapublishing.com

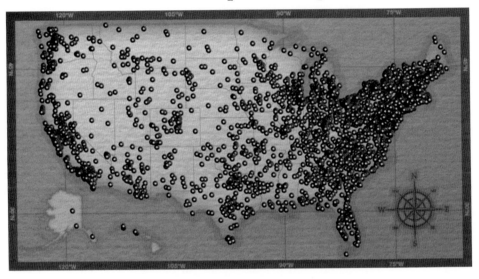

Search for your hometown history, your old stomping grounds, and even your favorite sports team.

978.701 W
Watry, Elizabeth A.
Fort Yellowstone